growing distant; coming closer

AF624752

Kianne Newton

BookLeaf Publishing

Presentation by *BookLeaf Publishing*

Web: www.bookleafpub.com

E-mail: info@bookleafpub.com

ISBN: 9789395969406

First edition 2022

DEDICATION

To my mother, who guided me towards writing this at all.

To my friends, who have always been cheerleaders of my writing.

To my family, who have always been supportive of my more creative hobbies.

Thank you.

candle

when comes the turn of the season, twisting time
around itself,
when hours stretch and shrink like the skeleton of
structure they are:
the seasons change and, with them, the people.
midweek, midwinter, midsummer,
unite at the midpoint, the centre.
seasons change and; as always; so does the world,
colour-shift leaves,
red-orange-yellow,
trodden-down dirt,
grey-black-red skies.
and every family settles,
finds familiar comfort in each other,
as days get colder,
nights get longer -
quiet nights,
soft evenings,
candlelight shadows.

sonnet to the subway

from the corner of my eye, a hunched-up shape
beneath the rails,
the shuddering wheels overhead, sparks on the line,
after it's gone, standing, rising, keeping its balance
with an outstretched tail,
a brief moment, overlooked, going unnoticed as if by
design.

something about the crush of people catches me,
the press of the crowd around my body, hand
clutching the metal pole,
part of my attention piqued, wondering what i don't
see,
whether everybody else is caught up in what makes
others' lives whole.

hot air comes rank, stale and still,
the wave of it catching unsuspecting passers-by,
it goes forgotten and ignored as each car quickly fills,
casting gazes upward to the unseen, concrete sky.

the overhead announcements echo like a code,
eyes heavy, late night, route lit as the dim phone
screen glowed.

ciiitrus

i stand under the orange tree at dawn.

where citrus sits in the air
and
where the vibrant colour is sharp,
is eye-catching,
is blinding;
i watch the sun rise
and
the night fade away.

i sit under the orange tree at midday,

and the sun burns bright above
to fend off clouds,
to bat away the rain,
while the leaves cast dappled shadow
over the book split open in my lap,
over my pale legs -
because i'm wearing shorts,
even if it's too late for it now.

i rest under the orange tree at dusk.

the sun dips its head
in welcome to the approaching night,
the wind picking up as
they make way for the cool air.
i close my eyes
and welcome the dark
as it rolls in around me.

coltrane

six times mother-of-pearl
imagined images of it, authenticity elusive until i
close my eyes.
far-off, the illusion exists - up close,
the veneer shatters and truth is revealed
in exposed and dirty brass.
what it is -
what it is, for me, is easier than words,
chipped lacquer a language i speak more fluently than
english.
no need to consider where adjectives fit or to ponder
the presence of nouns;
i take a breath; i exhale, i stake my claim on a
notehead.
i take a breath, i hold, i exhale - the familiarity of
motion,
there is a routine and so i fall into it.
inhale, exhale, breathe, move,
black ink on white pages that spell out technicalities
that needs must be spun out into art.

in absentia

it's the time difference that gets me, first of all.

i wake up to a phone call, the cheerful voices of my
family.
celebratory, even, and i'll admit in confidence
-
my sleep-addled brain has no idea what for
-
before something clicks.
the clock turns over, i slide into wakefulness.
happy graduation day, i say in reply.

i am missing the celebration.
i have missed the celebration, but I pull myself to the
side of the path,
turn my gaze down to the screen,
watch the people i've known for years crossing the
stage in black, in green,
and the faces all blur into one.

is she okay, someone asks the friend with a hand on
my shoulder.
she's watching her graduation, the friend replies.

people suspect, i think, that i'm mourning.
that i feel hollow, or that i'm missing something.
in truth, all that aches is the pride in the space
between my ribs,
that my friends and I made it,
that we scraped ourselves up to this point.

they call it, in absentia, for those that couldn't make
it.
they call me, my family do, and congratulate me for
the sleepless nights and exhaustion,
the rush of picking apart stories to their bare bones.

i graduate in absentia on a wednesday morning,
sitting out in the sun, and i wonder what the hell
comes next.

magpie childhood

call it what you will,
but i'd call mine a magpie childhood,
eyes always open and sticking on the newest,
shiniest thing around,
on the glitter of pennies on pavements,
and the way a family flocks together,
and the,
and,
and the rhyme isn't what it says,
no "one for sorrow" here,
because loneliness was peace,
solace found in the boughs and branches.

birdwatching

if i'd ever exercised any amount of forethought, i
might've asked,
(quietly, politely)
if my grandfather could possibly be so kind as to let
me borrow the book, please,
(although i can already imagine his flat stare)
and, please, i might see different kinds, and how am i
to know how to call for them if i don't know their
names,
(although, i was once warned to never speak the
names of things i can't ask outright)

the first symbolism i remember learning was about
birds.
i was seven, eight, nine years old,
reading and rereading the same trilogy countless
times,
words sinking into my mind:
birds are freedom, birds are the sky, birds are
wanderlust and adventure and exploring and -

so;
my grandfather's birdwatching book was left behind,
in the first drawer of his small table, where it's sat for
as long as i remember,
and i was left with the powerful tools of my eyes
(which are, of course, in perfect working order)

a phone that runs out of battery too quickly to be
much use,
and a shoddy internet connection that is, surprisingly,
unhelpful
(especially if the only question you have for it is
"brown bird in trees help please")

first of all, there are more geese than you know what
to do with.

i have a healthy respect for them, i'd say,
largely out of the acknowledgement that they're
living their own lives,
but also the fact that they're damn scary, and i may be
three times their size,
but i don't doubt that one of those things would make
a damn good attempt at goring the hell out of me.

secondly, the pigeons.

a staple; big city birds, flocks of grey,
as though they were stormclouds settling down closer
to the dirt.
everybody knows pigeons,
and so they go unnoticed, save for the cooing, the
occasional rustle of feathers as they take off,
as they land,
as they preen themselves in a search for
unappreciated presentability.

third, ravens.

a private observation.
early morning, the chill just barely lingering before
the humidity of the day burned it off,
watching a brown rabbit and a digital clock
rather than a white one and a pocket watch,
black shapes against an almost-white sky.

fourth,

and fifth, and sixth, and seventh, and eighth-

well,

they're why I wanted the birdwatching book.

most impressive, the finale,

there is a hawk.
impressive, still, unmoving and imposing,
it hovers above the low buildings and surveys the
ground,
the hustle, the bustle,
crowds below that look up and watch it in return.

the thing is, i could quantify a day, a week, a month,
in terms of exploration, of adventure.

in terms of birds.

proud

there's a lot going on.

everything is a rush of colour, singing and dancing,
is a rush, a thrill.
i turn to my friend and can't hear what she says over
the music that bursts from the speakers -
and so, she can't hear me in return, either -
but by the look in her eyes, she is laughing,
shares in the rush of belonging we can both feel.

the thing about a celebration in the big city,
the things they forget to tell you about them,
is that they're really,
really,
sweaty.
we tie fabric in a knot around our necks, have them
flowing out behind us as we join the crowd,
as we squeeze through the streets,
as we laugh and sing,
as we feel kaleidoscope colours on our skin under the
sun.

around us, there is bold, bright, everything.
are we part of it - we are, now, wrapping ourselves in
a blanket of familiar, familial, warmth.
we are here, everyone is saying, lost over the bursts
of music, and we are proud.

A List of Things They Don't Bother to Tell You

1. you will never feel like you know as much as the people around you do.

2. playing pretend was never something just for children

3. when you play a character too much like yourself, you lose yourself in them

4. a warm bowl of soup will make things feel slightly more okay than they are

5. you don't need to buy another mug.

6. no, seriously, stop buying mugs.

7. you will not magically understand all the workings of the world when you turn twenty-one.

8. if in doubt, call your parents

9. no, you won't ever forget the time you got yelled at in swimming lessons when you were four.

10. that as soon as you sit down to write a list, you forget everything about everything.

pre-destined

There is a thin line between weird and beautiful
and it is -

It blurs in the space,
fading into lights.

And there are lights;
there are always lights,
ceaseless and watching,
light years away.

Light years are distance, not time.
But time -
time is like wax, dripping from a candle flame.

It becomes the past,
becomes prologue,
while the future unfolds as epilogue.

Humanity,
people.

We recognise time.
We fear time.
We welcome it.
We fear change,
we envy it.

We search for something greater and,
by god,
it scares us.

We have nothing to fear
except ourselves.

We are unholy and awful people.

First comes love.
Then comes marriage.
Then comes the collapse of humanity.
Then comes the dissolution of the sun.

So it goes.
We know the story.
We have all heard this one before.

to a changing world

head-over-heels at half-past six at night,
and all that can be done is accept,
slowly,
that history is being rewritten before your eyes.

and the world is reeling -
as are you,
frankly,
and what the hell do any of you do now.

the country wreathes itself in black,
lets songs and cries of mourning
echo,
throughout the flooded streets.

summertime

what’s so sweet as a summertime friendship?
the bond you forge when you go away for a week or two -
the one kid your age, and you sit cross-legged on a grass-covered trampoline,
bounce it slightly while your hair falls in your face
and she tells you stories of old-town ghosts.

her name was heather - like the flower -
and she had long blonde hair that reminded me of fields outside the city,
of daffodils in the early spring,
of the sun when you squint at it in just the right way.
she wore a white dress and white trainers,
left by the side by my own black ones as we lay on our backs and watched the clouds.

the trampoline was our meeting-place,
and i kept quiet about the little hut up through the overgrown weeds,
let it stay hidden at the base of the tree like the secret it so clearly wanted to be.
we watched the birds wander the farmhouse garden.
will we stay friends, one of us asked,
yes, the other said,
but, like the warmth at the turning of the seasons,
well, you can guess how this story ends.

liminal space

fluorescent lights linoleum floors
city-block shelves faceless crowds
price tags blur countless produce
cart stacked high higher highest
full, heavy heavier heaviest.

come back to yourself
squeak of rubber soles on floors
condensation on fingers
stinging eyes
and you pass through the people, anonymous,
longing for the fresh air
beyond the dirty glass of the windows.

do you see how every inch of it looks the same?
technicolour packaging somehow blends into one
mass of it, every item the same,
indistinguishable.

and time, too,
time is given the same treatment,
every moment becoming a minute
extended, drawn-out, long-winded.
how long have you been here, you wonder
with what is perhaps your last coherent thought.

forever, the masses whisper back to you, and not at
all.

the worst thing a woman can do.

what you do is this:

you cradle her face between your hands and leave crimson streaked across her cheeks as you lean in to press your foreheads together.
you hold her close and then you move, hold the back of her neck while you breathe - in, out, in, out - and reach down to your side.

what you pick up, pick out, is small and just as red as your fingers, as her cheeks.
the juice mixes with the stains already there until you aren't certain what's paint and what's sugar.

you press the fruit to her lips and she bites down, sharp teeth sinking into soft flesh before she chases it with her tongue, cleaning a line of it from the length of your fingers.
you meet her eyes and they crease at the corners in a grin the likes of which you've never seen on her face before.

she smiles and she leans in close once more, says nothing, but presses her lips to yours.
there's something lingering on them that's sweet, that's sharp, that's sour and bitter, and you lean in again and again and again to chase it.

this scene, this tableau you've created, feels wrong to its core - it feels taboo, as though none of it should exist at all, and it's all you can do to fight off the shame crawling up your back.

what you do is this: try to force down the flush high in your cheeks while shame and guilt sink their claws into you; try to live in the moment and not to think about whatever repercussions might exist beyond this space.

what does it say, that your desire - that the simple act of wanting something is seen as something to be ashamed of?

the worst thing a woman can do is want, you tell yourself while staring at your reflection.
is that out of shame at what your desires are, or the fact you have them in the first place?
why is it that your desires have taken the shape of something with sharp teeth and claws, that takes names literally - it's called a ribcage, after all - and gnaws at the bars of the prison it's found itself in.

the worst thing a woman can do is want, and so i think, want on.

freedom

tell me, young thing,
do you dream of the sea?

can people see the spark in your eyes,
the promise of hope and adventure
somewhere behind them?
do they feel your love
as you bring them into your fold,
as they become family?

do you know the open sea -
do you feel its rocking beneath you,
waves almost like a cradle,
a promise writ in the deep blue?

and is there freedom still on the horizon,
while you curl on the deck
and stare at where sky meets water?
the clouds above part
while you move over
the currents and undertows,
while you gaze out and watch
the birds that fly overhead.

one night

so it's one night and you're curled up huddled in one corner of the couch with your knees up to your chest and a cup steaming on the table beside you; it's a weekday, it's a weekend, it's every day and no days at all, it's routine and repetition and part of your ordinary life.

so, it's one night and you're still high on life and the excitement that buoys you up from the day before; and it's warm, sticky in the heat; and you can feel your clothes clinging to your damp skin while you walk, while you laugh, letting burnt-out streetlights guide your way home.

so - it's one night and you're in a club surrounded by people smelling somewhere between booze and sweat and perfume; there's glitter falling around you like the rain from outside, there's body heat at your back and front and sides, your drink is half-empty from jostling and it leaves your hand sticky and shiny with liquor.

so. it's one night and you're sitting up late watching the storm blow in out of your bedroom window and the sky's a dark grey, black, rain hitting the window and running down it while thunder rolls overhead and lightning cracks the sky; it's later than you should be awake but what does it matter, when you can lean out and let summer-warm rain run down your bare arms just by letting them dangle outside, beyond the safety of the double-glazing.

it's a little...

the old broken-spine books of your childhood are
burning, now, and your hands shine under the
light of the moon while whatever clings to them
seems to absorb all of that brightness, leaves
them dark and sticky in a way you suspect
won't be washing off anytime soon.

it's a little funny.

smoke-smell reminds you of growing up all
while you leave it to go up in flame, embers
catching on whatever remnants of it are left
and leaving something acrid in the air that
mixes with the mire and mud and somehow,
there is dirt clinging beneath your fingernails
and tilled earth thirty feet away.

it's a little hazy.

there's something in the wind that strikes you
as unusual, a chill working its way beneath
your jacket, your layers, not quite winter and
not exactly autumn yet, the last days of summer
that fall away around you while the last
thunderstorms take their throne overhead,
leave you soaked to the skin and the fire only
still going thanks to thick pine boughs.

it’s a little late,

and as you walk home from this cremation
you think that maybe it could also be called
a creation, something springing from the
ashes; call it a phoenix, call it a shade,
call it what you will, but it walks
alongside you, matching each
of its steps to your own.

hunger

the first cut of the knife is easy.
it slices through,
rends, parts, separates,
two halves fall away from the whole.
the juice runs down the blade
before you lift it to your mouth,
chase the bead of it with the tip of your tongue.
the fruit sits on the plate
in a pool of its own redness,
puddling below it and
staining the ceramic.

or, perhaps;
it cuts through pale-pink flesh
to prepare it before it cooks off in the pan,
before its juices coat it in savoury
saltiness.
each cube shrinks with the heat,
browns, burns,
and you watch as it turns,
impassive.

maybe, still;
you sit the apple on the cutting board
and peel it,
skin laid out in thick, wavering curls by its side.
before you chop it into thick wedges,
cradle it between sticky fingers

as you coat it in sugar,
in spice,
and forgo the niceties.
it bakes,
it burns,
and you watch the caramel bubbles
turn black between pastry strips.

rules

there are rules for these conversations.

first:

do not lie,
for they will always know,
can hear the tremor in your heart that
betrays your dishonesty even as your voice
remains steady and unreadable.

second:

do not accept
food or drink from them,
for it always comes with a far higher
cost than a simple payment in coin or note,
and one bite is enough to sign away
your very own secrets.

third:

do not thank
them for the things they
offer you, for that draws you into
a bargain, into a deal.
and a deal with them is one that
you will never escape
the debt from.

fourth:

stay polite when
you talk with them,
because manners make the man,
and your wits are all you bring with you
once you step inside their circle,
once you take their hands,
once you join their dance.
fifth:

never tell them
your true name.
this is the most important,
loaded and weighted,
because a name carries power,
the sort that you don't want them to
have over you,
lest you have a desire to dance
for them,
all your limbs controlled by
strings.
do you wish to become their puppet?
will you do their bidding,
at the sacrifice of control over
your own body,
locked behind the mask
of a smiling face in the
firefly-light of evening.

snakeskin

i'm watching the crowd,
made faceless by blinding
kaleidoscope lights.
i'm letting the applause
wash over me like the
ocean waves,
feeling adrenaline course through
my veins.

i'll call this ecstasy.

the thing about acting -
about living, really -
is that it all comes down to
pretending.

whose mask do you wear today?
whose profile do you press
soft and malleable
flesh into?

for who do you shed your skin,
let the old fall away
to reveal the new,
still pink and raw under
blazing hot lights and unending scrutiny?

once upon a time

they don their crowns,
lady of the lake,
lord of the land.
so take up your blade,
knight of the people.

coronation is a thing that comes
wreathed in blood,
as you pull your sword
from the guts of the beast.
you let it hang loose
by your side,
tip catching on dewdrop grass.

they call you, 'protector',
when what you are is
a body curated for imperfect
violence and hardened by
cruelty.
the edge of your blade bites,
steel rolling and chipping
when it hits against bone.

you kneel before the crown
and feel the burn in your shoulders,
the ache that comes with power
in its own right.
you kneel,

and you wonder
if they have ever
felt pain like this before.

'heavy is the head that wears the crown,'
so they say,
but the two figureheads
keep their heads held high,
the line of their throat
unmarked and unremarkable.

there is something hollow in your chest.
once upon a time,
perhaps you could have put a name to it,
but now it exists like a gaping maw.
blood stains your linen clothes a deep
rust-red,
seeping slowly from the edges.

your title cannot begin to compare,
you are no ruler of nature,
you are merely the servant of the populace;
you exist so that they may continue to,
you fight so they may not have to,
you bleed so they never do.

your sword goes unnamed,
but its hilt is a familiar resting-point
for your scarlet-streaked hand,
the leather of it cracked and faded.
what once was brown has now
stained darker,

sitting black beneath the divots
of your fingers.

the lord of the land tells you,
'there is a monster just beyond our borders,'
and you take to your room to don
your armour.
it weighs you down and,
you know,
that it will be your death sentence,
sacrificing speed and stealth
for the sound of steel on steel.

once upon a time,
you went unnoticed and unremarkable.
once upon a time,
you were a noble and gallant saviour.

once upon a time,
the night of the people rode their horse into
the tangling and black-leaved forest,
and they never came out again.
once upon a time,
the kingdom mourned the loss of their protector,
while the lord and lady of the land and lake
turned to their court to press a blade into uncalloused
hands.

www.ingramcontent.com/pod-product-compliance
Lightning Source LLC
Chambersburg PA
CBHW051751130826
49812CB00033B/1099
9789395969406